Young
Ben Franklin

EXTRAORDINARY INVENTOR, BRAVE LEADER

Young
Ben Franklin

EXTRAORDINARY INVENTOR, BRAVE LEADER

By Laurence Santrey and
JoAnn Early Macken
Illustrated by John Lawn

SCHOLASTIC INC.
New York   Toronto   London   Auckland   Sydney
Mexico City   New Delhi   Hong Kong   Buenos Aires

ISBN-13: 978-0-439-02019-0

ISBN-10: 0-439-02019-0

12 11 10 9 8 7 6 5 4 3 2 1   7 8 9 10 11 12/0

Printed in the U.S.A.

First printing, September 2007

CONTENTS

Young Ben Franklin

EXTRAORDINARY INVENTOR, BRAVE LEADER

CHAPTER 1:
Life in a Large Family

On a cold Sunday morning, bells chimed throughout Boston from the steeple of the Old South Church. The family of Josiah and Abiah Franklin lived nearby in a small wooden house on Milk Street. Early that morning, January 17, 1706, a baby boy had been born there. His father bundled up the newborn and walked through the snow. He carried the baby to the church to be christened. The child was named Benjamin, after Josiah's brother.

Benjamin Franklin came from a large family. His father had come from England with his first wife and three children. They had four more children in New England, and then his wife died. Two of their children died, too. Life was not easy in those days.

Josiah married again. His second wife, Abiah, was the daughter of one of the first settlers of New England. Together, they had ten more children. One of those children died, too. Ben was the youngest son, and fifteenth of his father's seventeen children. Most of Ben's older brothers and sisters were married, with their own families and homes. They did not all see one another often.

At that time, Boston was the heart of business and culture in the colonies; almost six thousand people lived there. Its port was the busiest one in North America. Farmers brought crops there to be shipped to other colonies or countries. Trappers brought animal skins to be made into clothes and blankets. Animals roamed loose in the streets, and people kept cows, pigs, and chickens in their yards. A boy could find plenty to do in the busy town.

Ben played with friends on a grassy area called the Common. Sometimes he marched around Fort Hill, imitating the red-coated soldiers of the British army.

When he was not exploring Boston, Ben explored books. He wrote in his

autobiography, "I do not remember when I could not read." At first, he read the Bible and books of sermons. His favorite book was *Pilgrim's Progress*, a religious story of a man's journey. The book was the first Ben had ever read with characters, dialogue, and an exciting plot. He was thrilled to find out that "the written word need not be dry and overblown."

Ben's parents were always busy. His mother did not only cook and clean and care for all the children. She also spun wool, wove cloth, and sewed clothes. She kept the books for her husband's business, too. Mr. Franklin earned his living by making and selling soap and candles. He was a strong man who could draw, sing, and play the violin. He was known for his good judgment. Visitors came to him often to ask for his advice. Friends and neighbors joined the family for discussions during their meals, and the children all learned from these conversations.

CHAPTER 2:
Moving and Growing

When he was six, Ben's family moved
from their tiny house on Milk Street to
a larger one at the corner of Union and
Hanover Streets. Next to the house was a
workshop for Ben's father. Above the door,
he hung the symbol of his trade, a big blue
ball. The house always smelled from the
fat used to make soap and the wax used to
make candles.

Besides its size, another good thing about
the new house was its location. In the center
of the business district, the house was also

close to a fishing pond and a creek that flowed into the harbor. From his home, Ben could watch tall sailing ships being loaded and unloaded. He dreamed of going to sea.

When Ben was seven, he taught himself to swim. He learned by reading a book called *The Art of Swimming*. He also learned tricks such as swimming while holding one foot, swimming with his feet out of the water, and cutting his toenails underwater!

One day, some friends of his father's gave him some money to spend. Ben skipped along the street, laughing as he heard the coins clink in his pocket. He was going to buy himself a new toy.

Toot! Toot! Tweet! Ben stopped and stared at a boy blowing a shiny whistle. With each shrill blast, Ben's eyes grew wider. What a fine, sharp sound! What a handsome whistle! He wanted it so badly he handed the boy all his money. The boy gave him the whistle in return.

Pleased with his new toy, Ben tried it out. He whistled all the way home. He whistled all through the house. He disturbed the whole family, and annoyed his brothers and sisters.

"Goodness, what a loud whistle you have," Ben's mother said with a smile. "What else did you buy?"

"Nothing," Ben answered. "I spent every penny on this." He blew another ear-piercing blast.

"You spent all your money on that?" his brother cried. "You are a fool!"

Ben's brothers and sisters began to laugh. "You could have had four whistles for that price," one brother said.

"Or a whole troop of wooden soldiers," another teased.

"Or a doll and a ball and a big bag of sweets," his sister sighed.

Ben began to cry and the family burst out

laughing again. Their mother made them stop teasing him.

Ben sat by the fireplace, sobbing. "What a fool I was," he said to himself. "But I will never do that again!"

Ben put the whistle away. He never forgot that day. At times, he felt tempted to buy something he didn't really need. Then he told himself that most of life's troubles came from "giving too much for the whistle."

It was a lesson in many ways. Ben believed that anyone who tried too hard for friends, fame, or popularity paid too high a price "for the whistle." He used this lesson to guide him for the rest of his life.

CHAPTER 3:
Studying and Learning

When he was eight, Ben entered the Boston Grammar School. There, he studied to become a minister. He was a diligent student, learning his lessons in Latin and Greek. In one year, he rose to the top of his class and was moved into the class above it. But at the end of the year, Ben's father took him out of the school. Mr. Franklin saw that many ministers did not make much money. He decided Ben's education was not worth the expense. He also suspected that Ben did not want to be a minister.

Instead, Ben was enrolled in George Brownwell's school for writing and arithmetic. Ben was glad to go there because Mr. Brownwell was kind, and he encouraged his students. Ben studied penmanship and arithmetic. He learned to write, but failed arithmetic. His father decided that Ben was not cut out to be a scholar, and after a year, Mr. Franklin took him out of that school, too.

At about the same time, one of Ben's schemes earned him a scolding. At the edge of the town millpond was a salt marsh where he and his friends fished for minnows. They trampled the whole area into mud. The more they fished, the dirtier they got. One day, Ben noticed a large pile of stones near the marsh. He knew they were meant for a house being built nearby. But they were so perfect for what he had in mind! He talked the boys into taking the stones to build a wharf to stand on.

The boys agreed that it was a fine plan. When evening came and the men working on the house went home, the boys began hauling the stones to the marsh. It took hours of hard work, but at last they had a sturdy wharf to fish from. They went home tired but pleased with themselves.

The next morning, the builders discovered the stones were missing. They also found the brand-new stone wharf.

The boys were tracked down, and some of them were punished. After all that work, the boys had to return the stones. Ben tried to convince his father that a stone wharf in the marsh was useful. Instead, his father convinced him that "nothing was useful which was not honest."

It was time, his father felt, for ten-year-old Ben to learn an honest, useful trade. And so, in his small workshop, Mr. Franklin began to teach Ben how to make candles and soap. Ben ran errands and took care of the shop. He watched his father fetch animal fat from a slaughterhouse. He hauled it home in a wheelbarrow and chopped it up. He threw the fat into a large wooden tub and melted it down into tallow. Ben stirred the boiling tallow, which was then made into soap.

When his father made candles, Ben cut and shaped cotton threads into wicks. He helped fill the candle molds with wax. The work was hot and smelly. Ben did not like it.

CHAPTER 4:
A Job of His Own

After two years of this drudgery, Ben had a chance to work with his older brother John. John had started his own candle business in Rhode Island. Ben told his father he would rather go to sea, but Mr. Franklin refused to let him go. His oldest son, Josiah Jr., had gone to sea. His family did not hear from him for years at a time. Mr. Franklin did not want Ben to follow that path. But he agreed that candlemaking was not right for Ben.

Hoping to find the right trade, Mr.

Franklin took twelve-year-old Ben on long walks through Boston. They visited many different Leather Apron men, as craftsmen were called in colonial times. They were given this name because they wore thick leather aprons to protect their clothing while they worked.

As Ben and his father watched, blacksmiths shaped iron bars. Bricklayers built walls. Glaziers cut glass and set it in windows. Joiners built stairways and doors.

Coopers made barrels. Turners shaped wood on lathes. Braziers made objects from brass. These hard-working people were turning Boston into a lively and prosperous city.

With every visit Ben and his father made, the boy learned more about the special talents it took to be a true craftsman. Everything had to be made by hand, not by machines. And to do a good job took time, patience, and skill. Later, he wrote, "It has ever since been a pleasure to me to see good workmen handle their tools."

At one point, Ben's father decided Ben was suited to be a cutler, a person who makes and fixes knives. Mr. Franklin changed his mind when the nephew he sent Ben to work with asked to be paid for the training.

Finally, Mr. Franklin made a decision. Ben had always enjoyed reading, so his father thought he would make a good printer. Ben was sent to work with his twenty-one-year-old brother, James. James had just returned from England with a printing press. He was ready to set up his own printing shop. Ben would become his apprentice.

First, Ben had to sign "articles of indenture." This contract said that Ben would work for James for nine years, until he was twenty-one. Ben was to work hard and faithfully six days a week. He had to keep James's trade secrets. He had to be honest, reliable, and obedient. He also agreed not to marry, drink alcohol, or play cards during his apprenticeship!

The contract spelled out what James had to do, too. He was to teach Ben the printing trade and provide him with food, clothing, and a place to live. He had to buy Ben a new suit on his twenty-first birthday. James was also to pay Ben a small salary during the last year of his apprenticeship.

CHAPTER 5:
Working for a Living

Printing was a difficult job in those days. Printers worked with tiny metal letters. To form a word, each letter had to be set, or placed into a wooden tray, in the correct order. Sentences and paragraphs were set in the tray, letter by letter, until a whole page was ready. Then the printer slid the tray into the press. He added ink and placed the paper over the tray. To print a page, he pressed a heavy wooden block down onto the paper. To make another copy, he added more ink and pressed the block down onto a new piece of paper.

As an apprentice, Ben set the metal type into the tray. He learned how to operate the heavy wooden printing press. He ran errands and did any other tasks James assigned to him. In a short time, Ben learned the business and became a great help to his brother.

Ben worked long hours each day. Even so, he found time to educate himself. He borrowed books from nearby bookstores. Before and after work, he read about grammar, philosophy, science, and logic. He read a book that told him how to win arguments by asking questions until the other person changed his or her mind. Ben also taught himself the arithmetic he had found so difficult in Mr. Brownwell's school. He amused himself by making up "magic squares" in which columns and rows of numbers all added up to the same amount.

Ben still enjoyed swimming. Once he
used a kite to pull him across a pond.
In those days, boys swam naked, so he had
to talk a friend into carrying his clothes
to the other side!

At sixteen, Ben became a vegetarian.
He thought eating an animal was a kind
of murder. A book he read suggested eating
a vegetable diet. He had learned to cook
a few dishes, and he ate very simply. Some
meals were "no more than a biscuit or a
slice of bread, a handful of raisins, or a tart

from the pastry-cook, and a glass of water."
He stayed at the print shop and studied
while others went out for their meals.

One day, Ben made a proposal to James.
"You are paying for my food," Ben said.
"If you give me half the money, I will feed
myself."

James agreed to this plan because it would
save him money. It was a bargain for Ben,
too, because he was such a light eater. His
diet cost so little that he was able to save
money, which he used to buy books. Ben
was always careful with money. He later
wrote, "Waste nothing," and he followed
his own advice.

Ben also practiced writing. His first
published work was a poem called *The
Lighthouse Tragedy*, about the recent
drowning of a family in the Boston harbor.
As soon as Ben finished writing the
poem, James set it in print as a broadside.

A broadside was a large sheet of paper printed with a poem, song, advertisements, or a political message. Ben went out into the streets of Boston, selling the broadsides. Because people were still talking about the tragedy, the poem sold well.

Ben followed this success with a poem about the capture of the pirate Blackbeard. This ballad wasn't as popular as Ben's first effort. His father made fun of Ben's poems, saying that verse-makers were beggars. So, Ben focused more on writing prose. He made an effort to learn new words. He taught himself how to arrange his thoughts in logical order, and he imitated other writers whose work he admired. He even turned prose into poetry and back again, just for practice. He read and wrote before and after work and on Sundays, his only free day.

CHAPTER 6:
Letters to the Editor

James and his friends published a weekly newspaper called the *New England Courant*. It was one of the first newspapers published in America. James set the type and printed the sheets, and Ben delivered the papers. The first issue came out on August 7, 1721.

The Courant listed the names of ships entering and leaving Boston. It also relayed bits of news from the other colonies. Sometimes it published the views of readers who sent in their own articles and letters. James and his friends often made up letters to the editor, signed with false names such as Harry Meanwell, Abigail Afterwit, Betty Frugal, Tabitha Talkative, and Fanny Mournful. Some letters criticized the government. Others expressed opinions on current events.

Sixteen-year-old Ben gained valuable experience from his work. Besides learning the printing trade, he picked up techniques from the other newspaper writers. His style became stronger as he practiced. Soon, it seemed to Ben that he could write as well as the older writers. So he wrote a letter to the editor. He posed as a middle-aged widow who had opinions on many subjects. He signed the letter with the name Silence Dogood. He didn't tell James because he knew that James would never print it if he knew who wrote it.

Late at night, Ben slipped the letter under the front door. James read it in the morning, suspected nothing, and was delighted by its content and style. He showed it to his friends. They shared his enjoyment and urged him to print it. Silence Dogood appeared in the paper.

Ben wrote fourteen letters in Silence's name, commenting on poetry, urging education for women, and giving her opinion on all sorts of subjects. James printed all fourteen, and the readers loved them. James was happy with the newspaper's success, but he stopped smiling when he learned that the Widow Dogood was really his clever younger brother. When James's friends began paying attention to Ben, James became angry. He said he would never again publish anything Ben wrote.

Ben expected James to go easy on him because they were brothers. But even though he was Ben's brother, James was also Ben's boss. He felt Ben should do as he was told. More than once, the brothers brought their arguments to their father, who usually agreed with Ben.

CHAPTER 7:
Breaking Away

Five years remained on Ben's contract with his brother. He wished he could leave, but the law was hard on runaway apprentices. Then the *Courant* printed some articles insulting the government. Such a thing was not allowed. James was arrested and thrown into prison. Perhaps because Ben was only an apprentice who had to keep his master's secrets, he was let go with a warning.

While James was in prison, Ben was the editor and publisher of the paper. Under

Ben, the newspaper was more successful than ever.

When James was released, he was forbidden to publish the *Courant*. He thought about changing the paper's name but decided against it. Instead, he cancelled Ben's articles of indenture and made him the publisher. In secret, they drew up a new set of indenture papers. But Ben knew they could never be made public. An apprentice was not allowed to run a business.

James wanted things to be just as they were before his arrest. He insisted that Ben was still his apprentice. Ben reminded James that he could not show anyone the second set of indenture papers. They had to keep the secret.

James knew Ben was right. If he tried to hold Ben to their agreement, he would lose the newspaper. This problem angered

him even more, and the brothers fought constantly.

At last, Ben could stand it no longer. He told James he was leaving the printing shop. James asked all the other printers in Boston not to hire his brother, and they agreed. Ben could no longer earn a living in Boston.

Ben decided to sell some of his books in order to raise money for his journey away. He bought passage aboard a ship to New York. On the way there, he changed his mind about his vegetarian diet. He smelled the fish his fellow travelers caught and cooked. Then he realized that larger fish ate smaller ones. So why shouldn't he? He "dined upon cod very heartily." Later, he wrote, "So convenient a thing is it to be a *reasonable creature*, since it enables one to find or make a reason for everything one has a mind to do."

In three days, he landed in New York. He was seventeen years old, he didn't know

anyone there, and he hardly had any money left. He went to see the only printer in town. The printer did not need help, but he sent Ben to his son in Philadelphia, a hundred miles away.

Ben set out on another boat, but a terrible storm struck during his journey. The winds tore the sails to shreds, and a passenger fell overboard toward the crashing waves below. Amazingly, Ben was able to catch him and pull him back into the boat. They spent a cold, wet night anchored offshore and reached land the next day. From there, Ben had to walk fifty miles to reach yet another boat. After another long, cold night of traveling, he finally arrived in Philadelphia.

Filthy, tired, and hungry, Ben bought bread from a baker and walked around town to explore as he ate. After a good night's sleep and a change of clothes, he found work with two printers.

CHAPTER 8:
A Lifetime of Inventions

In Philadelphia, Ben met other young people who were interested in reading and discussing books. They practiced writing and read one another's work. They talked about politics and the social issues of the day.

Ben also met some of the leaders of the town and the colony. The governor, impressed with Ben's work, promised to help him start his own printing business. At eighteen, Ben left for London with the governor's promise to pay for a printing press. When he arrived, however, he learned that the governor's promise was worthless. Ben spent eighteen months there, working for other printers.

Then a businessman offered Ben a job in a new store he planned to open in Philadelphia. Ben took the job thinking he would no longer be a printer, but the man died a short time later. Ben went back into the printing business. Eventually, he started his own company, where he designed and printed money. He also published a weekly newspaper called *The Pennsylvania Gazette.*

Ben soon married Deborah Read, the daughter of the man who owned the house where Ben had first lived in Philadelphia. Deborah helped him run his print shop and store, where they sold pens, ink, maps, stationery, and his father's soap. They had two sons, William, and Francis (who died of smallpox at the age of four), and a daughter, Sarah.

Ben and his friends formed a club called the Junto. They rented a room where they could meet, and they stored all their books there. This inspired them to open a library. Members paid to join, and the Junto spent the money on more books.

Ben continued to be a very influential man in the community. Along with his friends, he helped start the first fire department. The group pushed city leaders to open schools and hospitals, and they worked for better street lighting and trash pickup.

At twenty-seven, Ben Franklin decided to focus on himself. He made a list of thirteen ways to become a better man. The list included developing such virtues as sincerity, cleanliness, silence, and frugality. He practiced one good trait every week. When he got to the end of the list, he started at the beginning again. Much later, he wrote that he "fell far short" of perfection but was "a better and happier man than I otherwise should have been if I had not attempted it."

Ben won fame as the leading printer in Philadelphia and all the colonies. His most famous publication was probably *Poor Richard's Almanack*, an annual collection of weather forecasts, poems, and humor.

His interest in science drove Ben to begin experimenting, and some of his results led to inventions. In one famous experiment, Ben proved that lightning is electricity. In the middle of a storm, he flew a kite with a wire attached to the top. He attached a key to the kite string. When the kite and the string were wet, he touched the key and felt a shock.

The skills Ben learned on his early walks around Boston served him well throughout his life. He learned to use all sorts of tools and do all kinds of household repairs. More importantly, he learned how to turn the many inventions his creative mind dreamed up into reality.

Ben's first known inventions was a set of wooden paddles that helped him swim faster.

He built a rocking chair with a fan on top. When he rocked, the turning fan blades kept flies off his head. He also invented a musical instrument called the glass armonica. It held a row of glass jars of different sizes. As the jars turned on a spindle, he played them with wet fingers.

Many of Ben's inventions were more practical, too. With his bifocal eyeglasses, people could see both up close and far away. His lightning rod protected buildings from lightning strikes. The Franklin stove produced more heat with less wood.

But most important was Ben's part in his country's fight for independence. After he worked for the postal service, Ben saw the value of uniting the American

colonies. Ben Franklin was the only
man to sign all four of the colonies' most
important documents: the Declaration of
Independence, the alliance treaty with
France, the peace treaty with England, and
the United States Constitution. In his later
years, he served with distinction as the
American ambassador to France.

A most distinguished citizen of the world,
Benjamin Franklin died on April 17, 1790,
at the age of 84.

Index

Look for these other exciting

EASY BIOGRAPHIES: